BE A
DOCUMENT
DETECTIVE

Be a Speech Detective

Linda Barghoorn

Crabtree Publishing Company

www.crabtreebooks.com

BE A DOCUMENT DETECTIVE

Author: Linda Barghoorn

Series research and development: Reagan Miller

Editorial director: Kathy Middleton

Editors: Janine Deschenes, Reagan Miller

Proofreader: Petrice Custance

Design: Margaret Amy Salter

Production coordinator and prepress technician:
  Margaret Amy Salter

Print coordinator: Margaret Amy Salter

Special thanks to Sandra Big Canoe

Photographs:

Keystone: © Poppe, Cornelius: Front cover (center right),
p6 (bottom left);

Shutterstock: © Frederic Legrand - COMEO: Front cover (bottom
left); © Sarycheva Olesia: p6 (bottom right);
© Everett Collection: p12;

All other images from Shutterstock

Library and Archives Canada Cataloguing in Publication

Barghoorn, Linda, author
    Be a speech detective / Linda Barghoorn.

(Be a document detective)
Includes index.
Issued in print and electronic formats.
ISBN 978-0-7787-3079-8 (hardcover).--ISBN 978-0-7787-3094-1 (softcover).--ISBN 978-1-4271-1873-8 (HTML)

    1. History--Research--Juvenile literature. 2. History--Sources--Juvenile
literature. 3. History--Methodology--Juvenile literature. 4. Speeches,
addresses, etc.--Research--Juvenile literature. 5. Oral history--Juvenile
literature. I. Title.

D16.B27 2017   j907.2   C2016-907111-1
                                      C2016-907112-X

Library of Congress Cataloging-in-Publication Data

Names: Barghoorn, Linda, author.
Title: Be a speech detective / Linda Barghoorn.
Description: New York : Crabtree Publishing Company, 2017. |
    Series: Be a document detective | Includes index.
Identifiers: LCCN 2017007121 (print) | LCCN 2017008099 (ebook) |
    ISBN 9781427118738 (Electronic HTML) |
    ISBN 9780778730798 (reinforced library binding : alk. paper) |
    ISBN 9780778730941 (pbk. : alk. paper)
Subjects: LCSH: History--Sources--Juvenile literature. | Oral history--Juvenile
    literature. | Interviews--Juvenile literature. | Historiography--Juvenile
    literature.
Classification: LCC D16.14 (ebook) | LCC D16.14 .B345 2017 (print) |
    DDC 907.2--dc23
LC record available at https://lccn.loc.gov/2017007121

Crabtree Publishing Company

www.crabtreebooks.com   1-800-387-7650

Printed in Canada/062017/MA20170420

Published in Canada
Crabtree Publishing
616 Welland Ave.
St. Catharines, Ontario
L2M 5V6

Published in the United States
Crabtree Publishing
PMB 59051
350 Fifth Avenue, 59th Floor
New York, New York 10118

Published in the United Kingdom
Crabtree Publishing
Maritime House
Basin Road North, Hove
BN41 1WR

Published in Australia
Crabtree Publishing
3 Charles Street
Coburg North
VIC 3058

Contents

History Detectives

Have you ever wondered how we know what life was like long ago? If you could travel back in time, what would you want to discover? In this book, you will learn to ask and answer questions about the past.

4

What is History?

History is the study of things that happened in the past. It tells us how people and places have changed over time. **Historians** are people who study history. We do not have time machines that can help us travel back in time. So historians search for clues to help answer questions about the past. They are like detectives who solve history mysteries such as:

- **How did people live long ago?**
- **How did an important leader's actions change the world?**

Learning about the past can help us better understand the world around us today.

What are Primary Sources?

Historians use primary sources to look for clues about the past. Primary sources are records created by people during a certain time in history. Primary sources give **eyewitness** information about people, places, and events.

Clothing, such as this dress made nearly two hundred years ago, can be a primary source.

Speeches are primary sources. Here, Malala Yousafzai is shown giving a speech about education in front of world leaders.

6

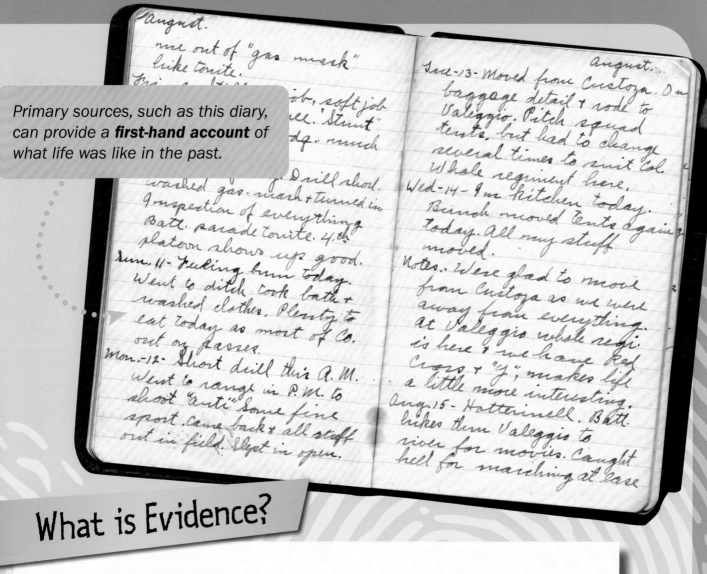

Primary sources, such as this diary, can provide a **first-hand account** of what life was like in the past.

What is Evidence?

Speeches, diaries, and even an old uniform or dress are all primary sources that can provide clues for historians. Historians use information from these primary sources as **evidence** to help learn about the past. Historians collect and arrange this evidence just like puzzle pieces to create a picture of the past.

Speeches, Oral Histories, and Interviews

Some types of primary sources are spoken. They include speeches, **oral histories**, and interviews. Often they are **recorded**. To record means to write down or tape someone's words. This means we can read, watch, or listen to them many years after they were made. For example, you could record an **interview** by writing down the person's answers. You could also record the interview on video using a camera or a phone.

Detective Duty!

As you read this book, notice the ways that the speeches, oral histories, and interviews are recorded. How would you choose to record a speech, oral history, or interview?

Different Sources

Speeches, oral histories, and interviews give us one person's feelings and **opinions** about an event they were part of. People at the same event may have very different experiences. So it is always important for document detectives, like you, to study many different primary sources.

We can learn a lot about the past from speeches, oral histories, and interviews. For example, your grandmother's stories about her childhood share what life was like years ago.

Speeches

A speech is a talk that someone gives to an **audience**. Usually, speeches are written first so the speaker can practice what they want to say. People give speeches to share information. They can encourage an audience to act or think in a certain way. A city leader may make a speech to encourage people to get involved in a community event. Studying speeches can help us learn about people who had power in the past, such as city leaders or presidents. Their speeches help us answer questions, such as what kinds of changes did they want to make?

Kids give speeches, too! This girl is giving a speech to her classmates to convince them that she would be a good class president.

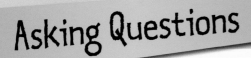
Asking Questions

When studying speeches, historians must listen to or read the whole speech. They can't use only quotes or parts of it. Using the whole speech helps them understand the **context** of the speech and why the speaker is giving it. They begin by asking questions like:

- **When was the speech given?**
- **What was the event or occasion?**
- **Who was the audience?**

How to be a Speech Detective

On November 4, 2008, Barack Obama made a victory speech after being elected president. He made his speech in front of a large crowd in Grant Park, in his home city of Chicago, Illinois.

As you read this part of his speech, ask yourself:
- What is his message? How does it make you feel?
- What words or phrases stand out?
- Do any words or phrases create pictures in your mind?
- What does he want us to think about?
- Is there anything you don't understand?

After his speech, Barack Obama waves at the crowd with his family.

"And this year, in this election, she touched her finger to a screen, and cast her vote, because after 106 years in America, through the best of times and the darkest of hours, she knows how America can change.

"Yes we can."

"America, we have come so far. We have seen so much. But there is so much more to do. So tonight, let us ask ourselves—if our children should live to see the next century; if my daughters should be so lucky to live as long as Ann Nixon Cooper, what change will they see? What progress will we have made?

"This is our chance to answer that call. This is our moment..."

These words create a picture of voters casting their votes.

His message makes the audience feel encouraged and hopeful.

These words are repeated many times throughout the speech.

He wants the audience to think about the future.

Who is Ann Nixon Cooper?

Detective Duty!

Use this link to hear Barack Obama's entire speech:

https://archive.org/details/barack_obama_election_night_victory_speech_chicago

How does listening to the speech change your understanding of his message?

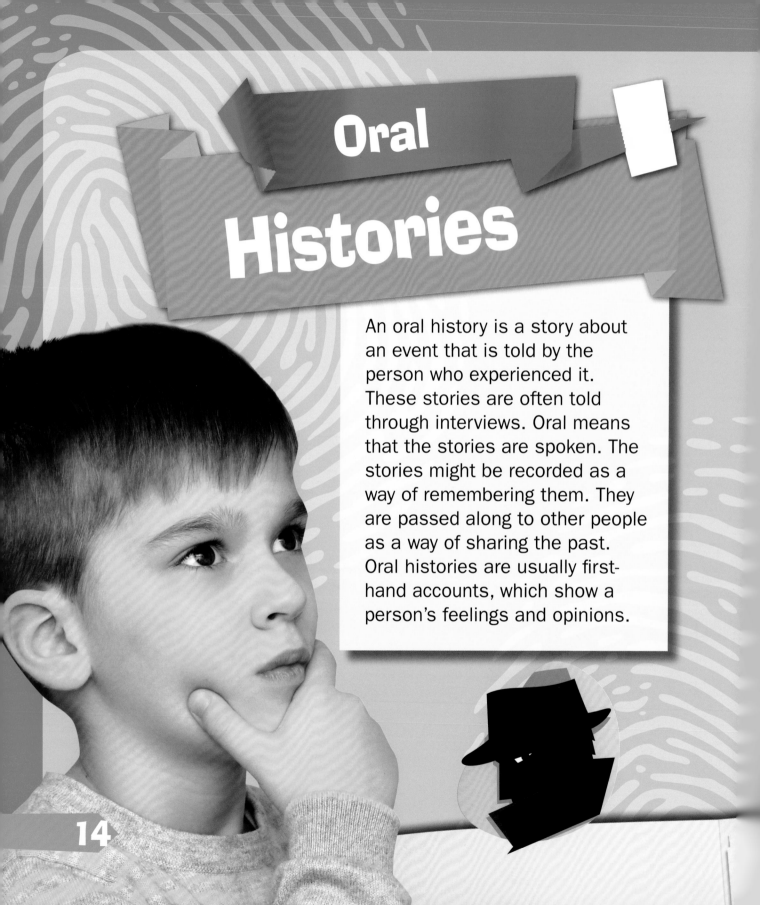

Oral Histories

An oral history is a story about an event that is told by the person who experienced it. These stories are often told through interviews. Oral means that the stories are spoken. The stories might be recorded as a way of remembering them. They are passed along to other people as a way of sharing the past. Oral histories are usually first-hand accounts, which show a person's feelings and opinions.

Asking Questions

Historians want to know why a story is important to a person, a family, or a community. When reading or listening to an oral history, history detectives ask questions such as:

- Who told the story? What can we learn about the storyteller?
- Why did they tell the story?
- When did the story take place?
- Where did the story take place?
- What can we learn about the family or community that was present in the story?

How to be an Oral History Detective

Some **Indigenous** peoples tell oral histories to pass on information about their history, culture, and ways of life. This story is an example of an oral history from the Chippewas of Georgina Island First Nation in Canada.

This photograph shows Lake Simcoe and Georgina Island today.

Surviving the Trip across Lake Simcoe / by Sandra Big Canoe

It was a warm summer day on May 30th, 1985. My eight-year-old daughter, Donna, and I [...] were on the mainland, getting ready to catch the little ferry service to Georgina Island. The school children that attended school in town were catching the ferry too. There were about twenty-five people crowded on the ferry with their groceries.

[...] We had already started out when the rain began. Thunder started to rumble in the sky. [...] The rain was so heavy, we could not see two feet in front of us. The boat was rolling from side to side and I thought we would tip over and drown.

It seemed like an hour, but it was actually only a few minutes before the terrible storm passed. We were all scared and soaking wet, but grateful to have survived. Most of the community was waiting for us on shore as we neared the island dock.

[...] Every family on the island had a member on the boat that day. What a near tragedy! Sometimes it takes a close call like this to make you realize how precious our home and community is to us.

Sandra Big Canoe told this oral history. She lives on Georgina Island in Lake Simcoe.

This event happened during the summer, when the lake is not frozen.

The event took place on the mainland, on a boat, or ferry, in Lake Simcoe, and on Georgina Island.

The Georgina Island community is small. Many people ride a ferry from the island to the mainland to buy groceries or to attend school.

Sandra wants to teach others about the importance of her community.

Detective Duty!

Visit this link to read the whole story:

http://georginaisland.com/writing/ surviving-the-trip-across-lake-simcoe/

What new details did you learn when reading Sandra's whole story?

Interviews

An interview is usually between two people. One person—the interviewer—asks questions. The person being interviewed answers the questions. Their answers can tell us a lot about their personal experiences, feelings, and opinions. The interviewer should prepare questions before the interview. Preparing questions helps them learn the most important information about the person they are interviewing.

Interviewers can write down the answers or record the interview on video to listen to or watch later.

Interviews can teach us about life in the past. They can also teach us about things that affect our lives today.

An interview with a grandparent can help us learn how our lives are the same and different from someone who grew up long ago. An interview with a mayor can tell us about how the important decisions they make may affect our lives. Imagine how different your questions to each of these people would be!

My Interview with Grandpa Santos

1. What was your favorite game to play when you were my age?

2. What was your favorite subject at school?

3. How did you help out at home? What chores did you do?

YOU!

The Incredible Interviewer!

An interview should give a person the chance to share their first-hand accounts of events and details in the past, and explain why their accounts are important to them. An interviewer's job is to be curious, ask questions, and listen. Today, you are going to learn to be an incredible interviewer!

Your Mission:

Find out about how the lives of kids in the past were different from kids' lives today.

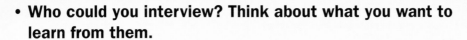

- Who could you interview? Think about what you want to learn from them.

- What kind of questions will help you with your mission? Use the examples below to help get you started. Then write five questions of your own.

- What will you use to record the interview? You might use a video camera to record the interview so the audience can watch it. You may use a voice recorder so the audience can listen to the interview. You could also use a pencil and paper to write down the person's answers. The audience can then read the interview.

What kind of toys did the person play with?

What did the person like to do on the weekends?

Did the person walk or take a bus to school?

That's a Wrap!

Once your interview is complete, share it with the class. Read the questions below and share your answers to show what you learned.

Detective Duty!

- **What did you learn about how the lives of kids have changed?**
- **What did you learn about the person you interviewed?**
- **How did the person's stories make you feel?**
- **What was the most interesting thing you learned during the interview?**
- **Do you think another person might have a different point of view?**
- **Who else could you interview to learn more?**

Learning More

There are many places you can visit to find out more about primary sources. Start with your local museum and library. Churches, community groups, and schools are also good places to find information.

These books and websites will help you learn more:

Books

Bruno Clapper, Nikki. *Learning about Primary Sources.* Capstone Press, 2016.

Fontichiaro, Kristin. *Find Out Firsthand: Using Primary Sources.* Cherry Lake Publishing, 2013.

Ingalls, Ann. *Isabella and Ivan Build an Interview.* Norwood House Press, 2012.

Websites

https://chnm.gmu.edu/cyh/primary-sources
This site includes more than 300 primary sources with information about children throughout history.

http://kids.canadashistory.ca/kids/home.aspx
The Canada History for Kids' site has primary source links, information and activities for Heritage Fairs, games, quizzes, and more.

www.thehistorymakers.com/biography/ann-cooper-38
Learn more about Ann Nixon Cooper's life and read about other African-American historymakers.

Words to Know

audience — A group of people who meet to watch or listen to something

context — Words that help us understand the meaning of something

evidence — Information that can help prove something is either true or false

eyewitness — A person who sees something happen and can tell us about it

first-hand account — A story or source, such as a diary, that came directly from someone who experienced or witnessed an event

history — The study of past events

historian — A person who studies past events

Indigenous — Describing a person or people who were the first to live in an area

interview — A meeting during which a person is asked questions about his or her life or an event

opinions — A person's views or beliefs about something

oral history — A story about a past event told by someone who experienced it

recorded — To make permanent by writing down or taping, either by video or audio (sound) recorder

Index

About the Author:

Linda Barghoorn has been sharing stories—hers and others—for years. She has interviewed rap musicians, TV news anchors, and most importantly, her dad. She is the author of several children's books and is working on a novel about her father's life.